READING SECRETS

READING SECRETS

A Queer Inheritance
of
Life & Scripture

Malcolm Himschoot

Flare Books

You can find out more at catalystpress.org.

In North America, this book is distributed by Consortium Book
Sales & Distribution, a division of Ingram.
Phone: 612/746-2600
cbsdinfo@ingramcontent.com
www.cbsd.com

In South Africa, Namibia, and Botswana, this book
is distributed by Protea Distribution. For information,
email orders@proteadistribution.co.za.

First edition, first printing
1 3 5 7 9 8 6 4 2

ISBN 978-1-963511-14-7

Library of Congress Control Number: 2024950738

"The outcome or the fruit of reading Holy Scripture
is by no means negligible: it is the fullness
of eternal happiness."
—Bonaventure, 13th c.

"Perhaps scripture also bleeds like Christ."
—Cheri DiNovo, 21st c.

Contents

Prologue

An introduction to me,
my ancestors, my children

The trees are sending down their sugar
    to the roots.
They are no longer sending up
    to the leaves new energy.
They have what they need.
Listen with me.

What I need, I need to say to my white
    children first.
Raised in church. Touching the Bible.
Listen with me.

My children, it is not anyone else's job
    to deal with our discomfort, our ghosts,
    something like guilt or rage we keep in our skin.
Generations injured intervene
    before another generation's injured.
The goal is something embodied, something real.
Dehumanizing disparity undone.

Food shared. Bodies healed.
One means to the goal is family stories
    shared. Secrets aired.
Anxiety becomes curiosity.
Curiosity becomes love.

What is at stake is not innocence.
We are not innocent.
The work must not start from self-deception.
God can do more with truth.

We must lose something precious, to find
    our souls instead.

So It starts with those who listen.

Part One

"We are aliens and strangers in your sight, as were all our forefathers." *I Chronicles 29*

A BIBLE STORY

How this all pertains to love

We give our attention to a story.
When the fire blazes up and the night sky
    descends, it begins.
After the trauma, after the separation
    and the genocide and loss and chaos, it begins.
"In the beginning." *Genesis 1*

My story:
My father died. He read the Bible
    in a certain way.
My dad died of AIDS.
He was a white Christian man in America.
When my dad died, I had feelings.

I too have read the Bible.
This is a book about the way I read the Bible
    and the way my dad read the Bible.
It was the only book he ever read.
Except those small tracts printed
    on soft paper and kept in his wallet.

I am a transgender man.
He never named me as his son,
    though I introduced myself to him that way.
That is a clue to this story.

When I was lonely, I tried to find my own language.
This is a little book about the Bible.

—

Stories of need and innocence, guilt and hunger,
    sensuality and prescribed custom,
    anger and hate,
    justice and injustice,
    life and death.
That's the Bible.
And also citizenship and slavery,
    longing and landlessness,
    government and insurgency.
In this lore, Love and Wisdom can be trusted
    and suspected in equal measure.
What is named might not be what is named.
Who is named might change their name.
God became Jesus, and Jesus became Christ,
    and the Spirit moaned
    and grew a church.

The Bible is that story, and ...

Listening, take a breath.
The story continues.

Somewhere along the way I heard a prayer.
I heard my own name
    and a name for God.

Jesus said, "I have no place to lay my head." *Matthew 8*
But we make nests and holes to smother
    and bury him in.
This is a little book about the Bible.
Big words may not fit.

—

The Bible is a place. People have lived there.
Betwixt, between, and beyond genders,
    people have lived there.
Around corners. In cracks.
Kept secret.

Some people find hospitality in the Bible.
Some do not.

If you stay, or if you struggle,
     you might belong to this place.
You might belong to this story.

—

Architects in every age design dwelling places
     for deities.
Big places carved out of stone.
A great canyon flipped above the horizon.
Canyons trace the etchings of ages.
Mysteries of water and wind write lines
     in stone all the way down.
Canons of literature scribe a monument flipped.
Sediments of writing stacked up on
     sediments of other writing all the way up.

—

My first Bible had my given name imprinted on it.

A name is a thing that is not a thing. A name
     can disintegrate faster than a gourd
     or a corpse or a rotten log.
A name can be traded like coffee or gold.
A name can be changed on a birth certificate,
     by court order, or in a ritual of community consent.

A name can inflate and then implode.
Can rise or fall like currency.
It can be two things at once.

Your identity might not be what you thought it was.
This happened to your ancestors too.
Maybe something promised is ahead of you.
Maybe your bones have meaning.
I had to change my name.
Someone told me, "Things will be more
    amazing than you've ever dreamed."

I read the sacred story again.
They were not wrong.

ANIMAL BODIES

My childhood and gender transition

In the end there will be words. Will there?
Always words.

It didn't start that way.
Recorded time started with words.
But before that, there were periwinkles.
Mollusks that change their sex in the sea.
And land insects, and birds.
Mammals with memory.

Then.
There were words, and then there were stories.
Proper names.
And eventually, obituaries.

—

Animate life.
The moral and amoral world.

Creatures that lick and wag and swim and
	slither and crawl.
In my first Bible, these were pictured.
In watercolors, pen, or etchings.
"God saw that it was good." *Genesis 1*
All good! All created good.
Redeemed by the rainbow when things went wrong.

An old family heirloom.
Spiritual DNA.
Was any truth from God there?
Words on a page.

The creatures got lost after *Genesis*.
Colorful murals faded
	in children's Sunday school rooms.
So did the enchantment of walks outdoors,
	looking down, nature-lover centers, aimless
	wandering, looking around.
Immanent awe.
I am six.
Time to grow up out of that.
Rainbows fade to moral judgment, the giving
	of law.
Vertical transcendence.

But always I remember the glory of the sky.
God's hands reaching down, cupped
    with blessing, to overflow on earth.

—

Lessons of distrust at an early age.
Breathing and stretching, dreaming
    and wandering, suspicious.
Too visceral.
Not wordful enough.
Mind?
That was something we had to do.
Otherwise, a spanking.
Subdue. Control. Dominate.
Lessons against, over, not with.

Verbs I learned. Objects.
Not to serve
    nor sacralize, belong among, behold.
Beware.
Not to revere the plants and animals.
Oblations, venerations, Native, immigrant:
    both foreign and subject.

What way of being is so suppressive, cursed?

There is blessing in the beginning.
And along the way, and at the end.
Every fall can rise again.
The living symbol of a cross forms a cycle,
    not a line.
Self and other in a circle.
God the sphere.

—

Animals reappear in the *Psalms*.
Sheep who rest.
Deer who long.
Birds who worship.
Animals tromp and slobber throughout
    the agricultural books.
Alive and also dead.
Goats are slain at the edge of town.
First fruits are sacrificed in the temple.

(Pre-words is wild.
Wild forms words out of worlds.
Words form worlds out of wilding wilderness.
Gender and sex belong partly to the world,
    partly to the wild.
Respect that.)

Animals lack significance for more than food
    if Adam's seed meant sin.
If judgment comes for the descendants of Eve.
If everything around you is the deceiver's work.

My father's world had gators.
Serpents and monsters and fish.
The big fish that swallowed *Jonah*
    could have been a whale.
Imagine!
Or say the dinosaurs were 4,000 years old only.
Say humans walked beside them and called
    them Leviathan.
This I am taught in second grade.
It made my father feel secure.
Adamant too.
To hold original truth, to be right, in spite
    of evolution.

—

Sometimes I still get triggered.
Sense and nonsense.
Signs like nightmares.

I carried myself above the neck.

Gender dysphoria.
Walking around with impossible dichotomies
    was good for me.
But it made swimming hard.
Unsolvable riddle: what to wear.
I bridged the distance between me and other people
    when I transitioned.
But unlike all those people in the Bible,
I was not allowed to change my name.

Transition was an animal experience.
Embodied, that is.
Skin. Scent. Hair. Hormones.
Nose hairs and sideburns.
Bathrooms smelled different.
Sexual impulses and body weight went up.
Cues to others went sideways.
I parted with breast tissue on a Tuesday.
The surgeon was used to dealing with women.
My friends gave me sayings and poems
    to read beforehand.
I pictured a spiritual place.
The body.

Gender means type.
But there are not just two, one menial,
    one celestial.

The great mistake of the West.
Hierarchical evil.
Scripture is more fluid.
Eunuchs and all that.
Powerful women.
Trickster men.
Not levels and mechanisms.
Spirituality.
Stories. Characters.
Children without a father.
A disciple without a son.
Jesus like a mother hen.
"My children, how I have longed to gather
     you under my wings." *Matthew 23*

This complexity of being animal.
Prowler and preyed upon.
Some of us pray annually for an end
     to perdition, mistaken predation.
Perpetrators: males, insecure of citizenship
     policed by gender.

Human animals.

I have knelt at the scene of hate crimes.
I have doctored the remains of the statistics
     of inequity.

I have smelled fear.

—

My father put fear in me.
Vexed and vexer.
Hexed by the Gideons.

When he first read the Bible,
    he had already decided to be militant.
To weaponize the text for subjugation.
Who taught him thus?
I think his father was involved.
Spankings going way back.
Preserve the seed. Revere the sire.
Men never touched their emotions.
Unblemished rectitude.
Taught not to listen, not to dialogue for truth.
To die rather than wrestle with authority.

I do still read the book.
My father's Bible.
Part curiosity, part self-defense.

I find things.

The cycle of forgiveness *Jonah* learned
    he learned from the plant that grew above
    his head, then died.
The cycle is the cycle of life.
Forgiveness is life.
Life is gift.

The cycle of gift is everything.

Spankings, cruelty, misogyny
    came from hierarchy.
Subjugation. Dominion.
Good luck with that.
Alphas depend on mycelium.
"Though they know not what they do." *Luke 23*
Utter dominance is utter dependence, and all
    is a cycle.

—

All the senses.
Touch, taste, smell, sound, sight.
Yes.
Miracles!
And pain. Thirst, hunger.
Proprioception, gravity. Loss, longing.

Desire, pleasure.
Inebriation or lucidness.
Sense of self.
Anxiety. Exhaustion.
Indignation. Shame.
Or simply the sense to urinate. Defecate.
An animal would.
An erotic, sensate animal would do more.
And marvel.

Human animals.

"Look at the birds of the air," Jesus said. *Matthew 6*
He said, "One of the flock wandered off
    and the shepherd went to find it." *Luke 15*
He said, "Not a sparrow falls to the ground
    without God's attention." *Matthew 10*
That's why he said each human could be loved.

Yet we don't have animals at funerals.

Desacralizing came first.
Then colonizing.
Racism. Sexism and ableism. Ageism.
Bias against pre-rational and post-rational bodies
    whose minds cannot compute.

My education did not have animals, but even
I realize. Dolphins do not do diatribe.
Our species does it so well, we've designed
    pulpits for it.
How words can slice and build and cut
    and corner.
Reach and wretch and seem to sanctify.
Loyalty and ruin.
Yet bees build holy hives.
Winged grouse drum the earth.
And dogs forgive.

—

My outward expression became masculine,
    if that means bearded and baritone.
The process of transition was feminine,
    if that means intuition.
Feelings. Blood.
Cosmic care for birth and care of the dying
    and touch for the dead.
Ritual with herbs and honor.
So many gendered places in-between warriors
    and water carriers.
Wise ones said there is power in
    transgression.

Making whole.
The power of connecting flesh and spirit,
    earth and sky.

Should anyone be that powerful?
Should anyone not be that powerful?
Jesus' words: "on earth as in heaven." *Matthew 6*

—

Other than Jesus, my dad knew no poets.
He was suspicious when I went to college.
He hoped it would raise my earning potential.

I studied nothing but words.
I tried to kill myself.
Suicidality a rite of passage.

In intervention, a friend gave me a cat.
The cat was with me until I came out.
Another rite of passage.
We were both homeless. The cat and I.
The cat did not survive.
I did.

A poem I wrote to my parents had cougars
    and wild dogs in it.

That year I made an indie documentary.
Another rite of passage: to educate on trans identity.
At the end, audiences always asked about my parents.
I could not give a domesticated answer.

We were undone, for a while.
But there's no us and them, with sexuality.
Dimorphic is not totally true.
Not even queer or straight, binary or non-binary.
Much more swervy.
Lines in motion.
Everyone is powerful.
Few hew to bifurcated gender roles.

—

Neither is sexual dimorphism total in the
    animal world.
Common yes, but not ubiquitous.
I say that not to defend my body—
    though such apologetics are a rite of passage—
    but to say the animals are kin to me,
    and so are the trees.
And so are they to you.
And so are you to me.

All is gift.

If we must fight each other, shall we fight
    as animals fight?
Not torch the earth at the end. Not fight to
    extermination.
But to rebalance.
Maybe even to welcome the other.
Life nourishes life.

Jesus' view of force: that love would take in,
    encompass, undermine, transform the enemy.
You are me.
I cannot hate you.
Because I stopped hating me.

—

Even your power I do not fear.
"Yay, though I pass through the valley
    of the shadow of death." *Psalm 23*

For sending me to ex-gay therapy,
    my father could have been criminalized.
Imprisoned.
That would have been a hell.
But no hell greater than he was already in.

My dad died.
So many kinds of death.
His remains are laid to rest in ashes
    in the Colorado mountains.
In the quiet.
In the wind.
Where the eagles call with piercing cries
    and sometimes a cougar.

Eagles call elsewhere too.
"A deer pants for water." *Psalm 42*
Dragonflies are older than us all.
Mushrooms turn up underfoot.

I am not worthy of the marginalia
    in the great book of Life.

Yet here is my heartbeat.

Because yours went before.

MUSIC

My dad's story of faith and childhood

He had several Bibles:
A large-print, leather-bound doorstop
    he used at the end.
The paperback that converted him as a young adult.
A chain-reference Bible, most familiar,
    from the middle of his life.

Along with his leather tool belt
    and his hammer, I kept two of these Bibles.
The first and last.
I sensed the secrets of abuse and oppression
    were there.
I knew the life-giving songs were there as well.

First, the Billy Graham version. Paperback.
It can fit in your pocket, but it has lots of
    extra text.
Before Scripture begins, note twelve
    MASTER OUTLINES.

Before you've even read it, it asks you to submit.
Understand a principle of dogma:
THE BIBLE IS THE WORD OF GOD.

Soundtrack: someone tying a millstone
    around his neck and dropping him in the water.
Splash.
I don't want to read more today.

—

THE plan of salvation is on page 240.
How nice that someone who knew it
    did not keep it a secret.
How nice they published it everywhere.
The problem: someone working so hard
    to save a man from sin, who is not that man.
Publishers. Evangelists. Preachers.
Dispense salvation as superiors would.
Formulaic. Conceptual. Contractual. Bought
    and paid.

Become saved, become one of the superior ones.

The other problem: who that someone is,
    spouting and selling salvation.

Someone invested in conquering land, races,
    territories.
The very definition of a man.

A bookmark in this old paperback Bible
    is no ribbon.
Tattered, durable, a strip of paper from airport baggage.
My dad walked the narrow way.
He did not drink. He did not gamble.
He worked.
When the time came for his firstborn
    to graduate high school and become the first
    generation to go to college, my dad
    took a second job.
Not to pay for tuition.
An hourly wage would not go that far.
He slung bags at the airport for a travel benefit.
So the child could see the family.
So the family could see the child.
What I know about the airport job,
I know from what was left in the laundry room.
Crusty pantlegs and scuffed knee pads.
He worked on his knees.

My dad's dad did not want to see his child.
He had no baby pictures.
My dad believed he was an orphan.

Growing up, he thought of himself
    as the black sheep, far from the fold.
He knew he was different. Not like
    his brothers, rough and tough.
He was supposed to be dedicated as a priest,
    said his mother.
He got as far away as he could from his father.
That's the part of the story I know.

The part I infer:
    homophobia was already in there.
Before my dad even had words for his sexuality.
Before he ever read the King James.

—

A Baptist minister became his friend.
Gave him this Billy Graham summary version.
Introduced him to the underlined parts.
The SHORT PLAN of salvation.
Made the story too tight.
Judgment yes. Righteousness. Faith
    and discipline.

Funny about this short Bible.
It's a New Testament only.
Plus *Psalms* are at the end.

The part where Jesus sings a hymn
    before Gethsemane is not underlined.
Nor Mary's song to bring down
    the mighty from their thrones.
The cry of the soul is not highlighted.
The flesh is only there for begats.
And corruption.

No peace is highlighted. Only war.

But FACTS are written in all caps. Page xxvi.

Everything sexual is underlined, and all of it
    is forbidden.
What my dad wrote in were dates.
"He who digs a hole falls into the pit
    he has made." *Psalm 7*.
A date hand-written in the margin.
"God reached down and drew me out." *Psalm 18*.
Another date inscribed.
And again another verse. Another date.
The pattern I recognize.
Suppress, repress, screw up, beg to cleanse.
Shorthand for forsaken. Shame-based confession
    where no one can see.
I cringe. Cruelty in private places.

—

I cannot be a child right now. No sublimation
    as self-deception.

Find me present, tense. Here. I wore this
    T-shirt to march in Washington DC.
"BELOVED BY GOD" it says in pink
    and white and blue.
My public alternative for queer masculinity.
Can small words help?
By then so many had internalized so much.
For context, I was not alone.
Thousands upon thousands of rainbow people.
We sang.

This is my Easter.
Rising up and overcoming.
Letting everyone know.

When I return to the text, I recognize
    a yellow sticky note.
Circa post-diagnosis. A pad of paper from a
    1990s drug rep.

—

Pianissimo percussion of pages in friction.
I hear men talking to each other,
     in a long lineage.
But I cannot hear their songs.

The songs I learned, I heard from my
     mother's hymnbook.
Assurance and comfort, love and praise,
     union and reunion.
"Rejoice, and again I say rejoice!" *Philippians 4*
No deviation? No!
Descants welcome.
Harmonies, always harmonies possible.
Rounds.
Undertones, overtones. Add percussion!
Music is a process toward fullness.
Wholeness. A new word
     for salvation I learned in seminary.
Deliverance and being spared? That's in Hebrew.
Wholeness, well-being, salve, spoke the Greek.

College was not a thing for my father or his father.
Dad graduated high school and got out.
Construction jobs were his ticket.
Someone always had a radio playing
     on the job site.

Country stations got reception.
Amplified, louder and louder.

It's possible my dad's friend saved him.
Or my mom did.
Or both.
Preserved his life again and again.
Before the dissonance did a number.

High standard. The straight and narrow.

All songs on the radio were straight.
But David and Jonathan was his favorite
    Bible story.
"Your love for me was wonderful, more
    wonderful than that of women." *II Samuel 1*

—

My father's next Bible was bigger.
It had a lot of text in the margins.
Extra columns. Concordance built right in,
    and more.
Like a Bible college course, or a series.
Haggai would have been proud of my father,
    the student.

His home, the temple.

But metaphors were lost. Literal was everything.
Hatred. Supremacy. You could actually look
    these up in scripture,
    and trace who was hating who.
Primogeniture.
Hundreds of words.
Thousands of data points.
Complexity. A publishing miracle.

The thing about this leather-bound Bible:
    it has such a long ribbon.
The flecks of gold are worn off the pages,
    which look like dust.
The spine is imposing.

"Never doubt," says a tiny fortune cookie
    inserted into the extra pages.
I look at my father's script.
The boilerplate. The end pages.
Of course he handwrote in
    the SIMPLE PLAN.
He had to add a list he numbered one
    through three.
Otherwise, the clear main point was missing.

The publisher included a map of
    "Jerusalem—Today."
The point of most maps: conquer.

—

I look up SONGS. A dozen entries.
Three citations. No notes.
A relatively silent word. In this long, long edition,
    published the year I was born.
Right before it: SON, SONS.
Two hundred entries. Many of them
    capitalized.
What inheritance did they mean?

—

Hagar cried. Rachel mourned. Jesus wept.

They sang in homes, in court, and on
    mountain roads.
They sang of earth and heaven.
They sang of soul and flesh together.
They sang of days, and days to come.
Release for the captives. Food for the hungry.
Being lifted up and loved.

The welcome that comes in the life of a stranger.
Creation!

These songs I couldn't unlearn if I tried.

—

I love the song that Jesus loves me
    and my neighbor
    with the love of God.
To that song, the Bible is a thousand lyrics.

But it's complicated.
"Build a wall, keep out aliens, and put your
    trust in princes" does not rhyme with
    "hospitality for angels unaware."
Compassion, courage, and the fruit of Jesus' Spirit?
Read between the lines.

—

Today you can buy a Bible designed
    in the color of your gender:
    military camouflage for young men,
    flowing pink for young women.
What hell is that binary?
Compared to whose heaven?

Soon after I was born, fundamentalists
    shrunk even Billy Graham.
"Love your enemies" said Jesus in *Luke 6*.
That's not what Focus on the Family preached.
Abortion was easier for someone to rally the troops.
Never mind the mysteries of conception.
Never mind
    women's own experiences, or how nature
    sheds a pregnancy in two-thirds of cases.
Justification of land settlement
    required white nationalism,
    and male domination conjured.
Female anathema.
If.
If you're a certain kind of white male.
(And everybody's got to be a certain kind.)
Virile. Resourced. Rational. Strong.
Universal. Superior. Normal. White.

Defined that way, you can choose
    to be a man or you can choose to be human.
Not both.
For humans are a mixed creation.

—

We sing to God with our soul.
We hurt one another.
We are rational and irrational.
We are confused and powerful.
We are vulnerable and frail, mighty and creative.
We are sensual and insightful, determined
    and aggressive.
We are particular and connected, linguists
    and lovers.
Archaeology might tell us this.
Or honest prayer.

Illuminations go missing in manuscripts
    purchased for solitary selves.
Responsiveness is needed.

That which harms is everywhere.

My father's Bibles refract selves
    who punished others for their own
    banishment.
Selves who propped up race as holiness,
    code for innocence.
Who hetero-sexualized everything, then said
    sexuality was bad.

—

Tell again a story.
Not for hollowness, but for restoration.
Tell again a story.
Or the toxins get too thick.

The story I love to tell.
The one my dad was striving for.
"Take my yoke upon you for my yoke is easy
    and my burden is light." *Matthew 11*

Christ, the living Word, harnessed no one
    without their consent.
Exorcised demons that yanked and spoiled.
Reached out to bless.
Designed a task that fit.

Jesus is living, not dead.
Something I cannot explain invites me
    to read more.
Truth beyond and between relational beings.

Listening matters.
Art and interpretation matter.

Poetic lyrics on the page.
Eternal striving in the soul.

Lavish rhythm in the body.
Trust the ointment.
Trust the song.

—

Jesus dissented about many manly things:
    eunuchs, for instance.
He preached *Isaiah* as a welcome,
    when he could have interpreted
    Deuteronomy as a curse.
"To the eunuchs I will give a memorial
    and a name better than sons and daughters." *Isaiah 56*
He said he had the authority to do so, to read
    and hear from God and understand.
A word of life, rather than a word of death.
"Rise," he told the girl others had given up
    for dead.
"Come forth," he told Lazarus.
"Unbind him," he told the crowd.

All the ways we kill and bind each other
    he confronted with life abundant.

—

These Bibles will not last always.
After my time they will probably be taken to Goodwill.
Or dumped in a dumpster.
Maybe they'll find their way to a landfill.
Or to the bottom of the ocean floor.
"Where thieves break in, and moth and rust
    destroy." *Matthew 6*
Non-eternal things go there, Jesus said.
Idolatry of the book belongs there.

I love the lamp that gives light unto my path.
But the lamp is not the Way.

—

My dad preached to himself what others
    preached to him.
Still, some radiance got through.

I know he sang "Amazing Grace."
His lullaby voice comes through to me.
A baby, infant, toddler me heard it.

Coercion too he preached, but did not sing.
Strapped and strangled music is mangled
    on a broken dulcimer.

Strains harsh and discordant.
Adolescent drama.
Teenage me asked for edges, bordered
 conflict, consequences to keep the world intact.
He obliged. Focus on the Family
 told him spankings were good.
Gays were bad.

—

A God who couldn't be satisfied except
 through violence—
 says the prologue from before I was born.
Before admitting
 the bible is a difficult book.

—

It's scary as hell to reckon with our lives
 beyond our control, truths beyond
 our understanding, evil behind our own faces.
But verily, the way out is through.

TIME

How my dad's life ended, and how I receive his
inheritance critically

Now is the pink-white-blue time of day.
You know the time. It's beautiful
    and will soon become lavender.
Right now, it is all hues all at once.
The liberation of night will come, then dawn.
Only after indigo, after coal.

The sun will be blackened for a time.
Don't worry.
Criss-crossed by shadow, clouds will smear
    the vision above.
Grab hold of something in the dark.
A hand.
Listen for a rhythm which is your heartbeat,
    for it keeps time as well as anything
    you'll ever know.
When you hear the rhythm
    and when you feel the pulse,
      then the flow of it all won't be so frightening.

A current passing underneath the half-globe
    of the sky.
Firmament above, firmament below.
And in between, only this shadow.
Now.

—

Signs and portents are in this book.
A final explosion comes at the end.
My dad told me.
But it doesn't.
He heard it linearly expressed
    from the dispensationalist pre-millennialists.
Somebody with a big name
    who gave him a small tract
    printed with heavy words on light paper.
These folks were certain when the end would come.
That made the Bible a watch, winding down.
A ticking time clock.
Revelation, however, was written long before.
Attend:
In southwest Asia a writer
    nearing the end of his life turned back,
    between angels and churches,
    to nurture glorious subversion.

No matter the cyclical nature of empires
    and doom, he coded faith into generosity.
This was the same man they say wrote a love story.
John.
Love is the word that appears most often in
    1 John, 2 John, 3 John too.
He was in love with Jesus.

Yellowed pages. Touched a lot.
He was in love with Jesus.
Many are.

—

My dad did not know that when you read
    the Bible, you also read about you.
Do not blame him.
He had learned a myth of himself.

He gave me my Bible when time was young.
I loved reading *Genesis.*
Playing and praying
    and Jesus loves me and pine trees and blue sky
    and horses and the road to the dump.
Adventure stories. Promises.
Childhood time. Eternity.

I gave my life to Jesus, and my heart too.
There was so much to give.
Love came from the clouds and through the
    waterfalls and filled up the streams
    that sparkled unending to town.
I grew up and read lots of books.
"The more knowledge, the more grief." *Ecclesiastes 1*
With much reading comes much suffering.

God might love me, but I wanted proof.
Time changed. Puberty and all that.
I discovered things I could not explain.
Maybe God hated me.

I needed to know there were people like me,
    with hearts that beat faster and slowed for … sin?
Voices on the radio said it.
The preacher on Sunday said it.
Sin was a large, sexual word.
Men spoke in diatribes, loudly.
Women told proverbs in a hush.

—

Forces act on us.
We act in turn.

There are moments we can't get back.
We decide every moment who we are.

—

I wrote an essay for the Daughters of the
     American Revolution.
It won a prize.
When I heard stories of courage and sacrifice,
     I decided to become a missionary.
That's what women did.

(If not for a transgender miracle,
     I would not need to write this book.
But someone still might need to read it.
Someone who has kept time
     by promised land and prophecy
     needs now to let go of apocalypse.
Each season is blessed.)

Look at the birds of the air.
Look at the lilies of the field.
Liberation happens in history.
There is something called proleptic eschatology,
     and the Christian year is a cycle.
That's the end run.

That's the shortcut to the future.
"Though it tarry, it shall surely come." *Habakkuk 2*

If you already know the Western calendar
    is a myth, by all means skip ahead.
Past the sixty-six scrolls forming a library
    of sacred literature.
Eurochristians poaching Asian texts preserved
    in Africa.
Past the someday threats that made me
    almost take my life.

If you need to read slow, read slow.
Time is all there is.
A vast fabric, like the sky.

—

I came out at twenty.
We did not talk for years, my dad and I.
In his view, based on eternity itself
    and things that cannot change,
        all hell broke loose and I was damned.
Twenty years later he was dead.
I was not.

When I came out, in queer community
    with sexual health education, it saved my life.
When he stepped out, it cost him his.
I was lonely and unsure.
He was miserable
    and condemned.
When he died, he left me his Bible.

—

All of this was broken.
Forever was a weight.

We were not taught sun or moon for telling time.
Even now, I need to study the light.

The year gets dark and starts over.
Every year so far, but only now am I paying attention.
Rely upon the dim, before it gets brighter again.
Some time is waiting time.
Twice a year, the Christian calendar says, "Wait."
In Advent, full with anticipation.
In Lent, empty with preparation.
I did not know about this, back then.
I did not know the seasons are blessed.

Is it possible to adore the end of time?
This extravagance of *Colossians* and
    Thessalonians.
Compared to the anachronism of polyester.

Once our family rituals marked patriotic dates.
Each Fourth of July was sacred.
History started in 1776, and there was no
    Christianity outside of America.
Somewhere someone was born again, on no
    particular saint's day.

The seasons were archaic.
Not like the lilies of the field.
Rather, collapsed.
Stick it in your purse and own it.
Instant Armageddon, all the time.
Stay on the path. The righteous do.
Lest you turn aside to the troubling matters
    of human rights, lest you glimpse
    the devastations of modern history.
This would be too much.

—

Imaginary time.
Past.

When I was a child, my dad was at his best.
He told childhood stories. I laughed
    and laughed.
He kept phone numbers in his head. I was impressed.
He used a carpenter pencil to scratch figures on wood
    and sharpened it with his utility knife.
I wanted to be like him.

Time is not linear.
That's the imaginary part.

Promised time.
Future.
We know we do not know what's coming.

Based on shame, based on failure,
    based on rejection, predict nothing.
If you could know it already, it would be past.
The future, you and I do not know.
Everyday intervention is a mystery.
It has come here before.

—

Maybe someone asks you a question, and it
    gets under your skin.

Maybe someone sees you in a new way.
Maybe someone shares the art of their life.
All of a sudden, possibilities open up.
Conversion. Solidarity. Passion enough
    to move tombstones and mountains.
What if?

Waiting is accomplishment.
It took me a long time to adjust.
I thought maybe closeted time was failure.
It was not.
I thought maybe coming out meant victory.
It didn't.
Sustain and overcome.
The twin recipe of liberation.
Repetitive ingredients.

You and I have no evidence for time.
No evidence for ourselves.
Yet here we are.
Before and after, gift.

Both hope and penitence come round
    and round again.
Reciprocity calls forth repentance.
Repentance, regeneration. Regeneration,
    reciprocity.

The scale of one lifetime is not enough.
So much from fathers to sons, see?
For this reason.
The seasons.
Many sons later, waiting will be full.

—

Comes more than once, "to every man
    and nation," the moment to decide.
Good or evil. Truth or falsehood. Virtue, vice.
Lyrics to a Civil War hymn.
But cyclical, repetitive.
In this world human migration meets tear gas,
    solitary-detention cells, decimation by
    reservation, continuing harm.
Injustices are repeated.
Causes do not prosper on their own.
People moved by Spirit get involved.
Show up.
Keep showing up.
Generations later, they may say
    it was inevitable progress.
No.
It was somebody's sacrifice and risk.
Somebody's reverent courage and compassion.

A word of accountability and
    a word of affirmation that
    called out a greater and a lesser moral cost.

—

Crack open time.
The fragments are all still there.
My dad was a teenager in the 1960s.
Hated hippies.
Since he wasn't responsible for the Civil War,
    he never said anything about civil rights.

Somebody taught James Baldwin the Bible too.
Baldwin would have been a preacher in the Black
    church, but he became a prophet to white America.
The times and seasons demanded it.

Perhaps I should not put James Baldwin in a book
    about my dad.
My dad did not know about Baldwin.
Baldwin did not become a dad.
My dad—if you asked him—was not gay.
But this is a little book about the Bible.
God knows what anti-racists were up against.

Christ knew the white man's soul.
Knew to reach back and keep going.

People in the midst of time.

—

Prophets in the mists of time.

Zechariah, Malachi foretell joy
    for God's people.
A little word. Shalom.
Means justice and peace. Truth and trust
    and self-respect.
Spirit and vision and abundance after the moment
    of decision.
They answer not the question when.
But why?
"Why" is repetitious. Like failure.
Like wound. Like healing. Like hope.
Purpose and struggle share this.

Neither tragedy, nor comedy.
But love without end.

Part Two

"I pray that God may strengthen you with power in your inner being." *Ephesians 3*

HUNGER

My story of seminary and vocation after transition

Hunger, like fire.

Licking, soaring. Consuming.

But nothing to consume, no strength, nothing
   to bite or swallow.

Rigoberta Menchú said, I read, "Hell is
   having no bread."

Jesus prayed,
   and the disciples were swayed.

"Give us this day." *Matthew 6*

Enough to share.

Bible stories were not written from privilege.

No way they would have survived ages
   and ages as a map to happy.

People did not have flu shots and penicillin,
   anesthesia or life insurance.

Take the temperature of Scripture
    and it smells like suffering.
Charred. Burnt.
Hungry people on whom the story hinges:
Naomi, Joseph, Elijah and the widow of Zarephath.
Mary, mother of God.
(Don't tell me pregnant people aren't hungry.)

It is profoundly human to register
    how the belly feels when it's empty.
To have anger, and headaches.
To lose focus.
To gain focus.
To deal with sugar crashes, high
    and low metabolism, the shits, dehydration.
Digestion is what we are made of.

People who have not known hunger
    might not read the Bible well.
Trust the ones who have had little food,
    and who have learned to share it.

—

Communion is no symbolism. It's heaven
    in the midst of hell.

A good meal is from the church food shelf
     when you're hungry.
That's my experience.
When one church kicked me out, another
     took me in.

Injustice drives up hunger.
Like torture.
Like a yoke that doesn't fit.
Like bonds too tight that burn.
You can recognize oppression that way.
Systemic wrong takes away food
     and freedom, resources and replenishment.
Injustice grinds down people to nothing.
And eats them.

Liberation, said Rigoberta Menchú, is bread.
Fasting is one way to remember.
So is feasting.
Both in measure.

There are other kinds of hunger too.

—

People say to stay away from desire.
But bodies are made for sex.
Best to know one's appetite and how to meet
    a need with gratitude and respect.
Best to ask permission.
And say thank you.
Hormones are hormones.
An entryway to relationship
    and all the lessons of sharing.

Contrast unchecked hunger.
Taking only, nothing to give.

Oppressors write their history in,
    or read it out.
Before my dad's dad immigrated,
    tracks were laid down for inhumanity,
    profit, segregation.
Exploitation manifest.
Hunger laid down history white over Black:
    sugar and rice.
White over Brown:
    peaches and lettuce and grapes.
Pineapples and bananas.
Railroads over Chinese.

When I grew up
    someone drove 26 nationalities underground,
    cooking up nothing but smelt from mines.
My dad's dad learned to put down labor.
My dad learned to silence dissent.
His own, when he was the laborer.

Scars on the sacred pages,
    justify slavery, violation, criminal usury.

My dad learned to stomach desire.
Swallow empty. Repress.
No olive oil of gladness.

—

But who is a foreigner, anyway?
Who is a neighbor?
Why does GOD—in the smelting, refining, drenching
    pages—continually call to a table of justice?

To nourish the soul, resist oppression.
Expose famine.
Do not kill, exploit, or assimilate.
Do not marginalize, denigrate, or dominate.
"You give them something to eat!" *Mark 6*
Make food clean.

Jesus cuts my words, and keeps calling.
Violence is not God's will.
Keep seeking.

To wait, past when waiting is good.
To consume oneself.
Or to breathe beneath a vine and fig tree.
Space for the sublime without repression.
Hunger and thirst for righteousness.

—

If you want a philosophy of religion, forget food.
Between rationalism and cult
    is a rich banquet of tradition,
      prepared and served by an indigent deity
      with mortal help.
Creator-Redeemer-Sustainer immanent to
    this earth.
Good calories, secure provision, source.
Connection, culture, lifeway, flesh.

A fire smells nice when it's a warm cooking fire.
The smoky smell of spices and juices and wood.

Jesus was a solidarity person.

Oxygen for the fire of the Spirit. Word of God.
He breathed, and they felt peace.
They warmed to his voice.

Often debating with scripture,
    like his ancestors he wrestled, prayed.
Prayed and read.
Read and sang.

Words on the page were not the Word.
No scribe could be deified.
The kind of church I had to leave:
    empty plates, and stones for spoons.
Jesus sang and fed people.
Oxygen makes a fire, fire.

Taste, and see.
Test, and hold.

—

In the belly of one starving person
    are whole structures of deprivation.
To conceal poverty, society metabolizes
    censorship.

When I was hungry, I was mad at God.
I lived in my car, I slept in my car.
I drove past churches and cursed.
This was my experience of being homeless
    and being trans.
Found out, kicked out.
It was good practice for something different.
Sacrament.

Epic hunger belongs not to one alone,
    but to a people.
Millions starving. Millions thirsting.
The ruined make a way out of captivity.
The valley where dry bones live.
Tears in exile restore.
Something about hunger leads to solidarity.
Heartbreak becomes heart, open to others.
The Bible can model this.
Jeremiah, Lamentations. Eviction.
Not an excuse to blame disreputables,
    but mourning itself.
A burning fire and a deep wound.
A spiritual move from moralism and tragedy
    to justice and dignity.

Hunger in the Spirit.
The Spirit like a fire.
Cooking fish at the lakeshore
    one impossible morning?
Recipe for change.
There is enough food, if only it is spread around.
There is enough time to gather, heal,
    and harvest.
There is enough for Zelophehad's daughters
    in *Numbers*.
There is enough for the Greek-speaking
    widows in *Acts*.
Miracles where the Spirit is.
Loaves and fishes for everyone.

—

The kind person who took me in
    was a church person.
She said, for a few months, until you find
    your feet again.
And other good words, but nothing too preachy.
I ate a lot of grits.
And peanut butter, bread, beans and rice.

—

My dad bought his next Bible.
Heavier, thicker.
We didn't see each other,
    so I didn't know it was large print.
But I could hear it through the phone.
Epithets and writhing.

I went to seminary and ate free pizza.
I was assigned a parish, where I ate bologna
    sandwiches with jalapeño.
My job was to make one big pot of pozole
    to feed a hundred people

Comes a comforter, an advocate.
My father was suspicious.
Why not require change, perfection first?
Something corrupt.
Something lavish.
Extravagant.
Like a meal with fine ointment.
Christ's affirmation.
Made everybody feel weirdly sensual
    and naked.

PURITY AND PAIN

How I felt when my father died,
and who to blame

Pity, purity, pain. Pain.
Rain.
Pity I feel for the way my father died.
Purity he sought.
Pain he died with.

My dad died in a deluge of purity.
He was persuaded AIDS meant God's
      punishment on homosexuals.
He did what he thought his father's god demanded.
My father rejected his gay son, and his trans son.
This was a sad time.
When I think about it, it rains.

—

"Detestable." *Leviticus 18*
The only line underlined in a whole book
      of covenant.

A single stroke to strike relationship.

The rest of my father's story is not told
    in the code
    of the ancient people
    trying to live for years in the desert.
They sought to limit disease.
The priests had the power to say
    who was "clean" and who was "unclean."
Clean meant free to move about the community.
Unclean meant sequestered, quarantined,
    or left outside.
Pork could transmit disease, or raw shellfish.
Science was known by cultish names.

Other abominations came later.

Deuteronomy, for instance.
Righteousness and group identity
    meant survival in the desert.
Those who followed the rules
    were identified as true children of God,
    and questioners or heedless of the rules
    were Godless people.
How simple it must have been.
Except the gender-blenders, rule-benders.

Even at that time—and in all times—
    "thou shalt not" commandments clue us in.
This or that was NOT the only.

Stakes were always scorching high.
Later in the time of *Daniel*, our hero
    dared eat no meat, lest it be tainted.
He was thrown to the lions.
His friends thrown in a furnace.
In exile, they walked
    through fire to prove they worshipped right.
God was God, and the priestly code
    demanded allegiance.
What was the small matter of sex?
Life or death, as always.

As always, some men had sex with men.
"If a man lies …" *Leviticus 20*
Priests did.
For legislating romance is a desperate measure.
In any desert, love is parched, and eros burns.

—

On the other side of wilderness lay promised land.
Good land for settlers.

"Have sex with women!" the priests
    told the men, nation-building now.
But not all women!
Foreign women were suspect.
Native women too.
Women who worshipped woman gods.
My father read this narrative
    as an Old-World immigrant becoming American.
Manhood got him through a drought before,
    and manliness purchased victory ahead.
At the cost of his soul.

Ancient warriors knew what the priests knew.
    Kings and *Chronicles.*
Intimate with a blade, triumphant men
    castrated other men after each border war.
Like rape in war, this was genocide.
Unclean, unclean! the priests declared.
Sex assault was more than trauma,
    but healing went unrecorded.
Lest everyone be a dry tree,
    non-castrated males who survived
    bore heavy responsibility.
I imagine they never got to wash the sand off
    their bodies and go skinny-dipping carefree.

Their days were numbered and rendered.
To the worship of war and reproduction.

Manhood was not deity.
Not everyone can accept this teaching.
Only "those who are eunuchs for the sake
    of the kingdom of heaven." *Matthew 12*
Yet ancient scribes scraped dry patriarchy
    into the Bible: *Timothy*, *Peter*.
Fear and terror of perversion in *Jude*.
Pages stuck together.
Masculine duty, sacralized.
Devout people trying to be good men.

My father got "born again" when he met my
    mother. They married. They had kids.
They found churches where it would not rain.
Searched out where no groundwater pooled
    in marshes.
Devotion and coercion sacrosanct on solid land.

Pity those churchmen rewarded
    only for duty, motivated by shame
    over love of the Lord.
Pity the women they loved.
Pity the ones who loved them.

My father preached at the dinner table.
When he was home.
He came home less and less.

—

The Bible hints also at matrilineal
    and indigenous wisdom.
Pleasure did not always mean immorality.
Immorality did not always mean infidelity.
Infidelity did not always mean impure.

But then heterosexuality and patria
    joined the story of the race.
And purity took command
    for a white man in America.

It killed my father.
His suicide was slow and gruesome,
    and grievous to his survivors.

Sometimes I take down my father's Bibles
    from the shelf.
The only book I ever saw him read.
Sometimes when it rains, I cry.

—

Missing from the list of impure: prostitutes.
Sex workers were fine.
They knew what warriors knew,
    and they knew what priests knew.
They knew all.
For more than one religion.
More than one nation.
A loophole discovered in the code-bound sexuality
    of a whole group of people,
    this one set of people,
    genderless, multi-gendered,
    was exceptional.
Morally? Ambiguous.

Morals are rules. Not cosmic, but a society's rules.
Rule-following is expected for all who belong.
Except for a few, who make the rules.
Exodus was the beginning-again,
    long after the patriarchs wandered
    famished into Egypt, and after their bargain
    for food became bondage.
With Moses' help they left
    through the Red Sea.
But on the other side
    his sister Miriam dared to question Moses.
For raising her voice in question and critique
    she was stricken with leprosy.

Moses' brother Aaron, for the same
      infraction, was given only rebuke.
A gender thing: rule-following enforced
      for some more than others.
The five books of Moses recount
      a long history of taking of power
      away from strong women
      and giving it to men.
This was all legalized.

—

I am not the first one to weep.

In the time of the patriarchs, women
      had to compete with other women
      to bear children for a man.
But any woman unfaithful to her husband
      was condemned.
This is the sad part of *Hosea, Jeremiah,
      Ezekiel, Nahum.*
God's voice is the voice of a jealous lover,
      and the love song is a threat,
      a tirade of abuse.
God is a "he" and the object of affection a "she."
If she is found impure, then he
      could become violent against her.

These are the rules of covenant?
These are the rules of marriage?
These are the rules of masculinity to the death.

The land was to be conquered.
The conquest is purported complete,
    so the picture presents purity.
But if it were pure, it would be sterile.
In *Joshua*, the land changed hands,
    the walls of the city fell.
But Rahab, the prostitute who lived in the wall,
    managed a sort of polytheism.
And survival. And sex work.
No one expected her to be pure.
She had license to switch sides.
She was the exception.
Then you read *Ezra* and you realize,
    there were a lot of exceptions.
A lot.
A lot of mixed-status families.
A lot of inter-ethnic relationships.
A lot of marriages
    generating lineages based on love
    that could not be mapped or desiccated.
The land, like a woman, is not there to be conquered.

—

Why do I read the Bible when it rains?
To wash the blood
    from the sand.

—

To the counterpoint of purity, a counter-
    vailing value.
Character.
Do not look here for judgment
and condemnation.
Look instead for pathos
    and tragedy, ethics over morals.
Some Bible stories do not end
    in a verdict at all.
Morality helps establish order, when order
    accompanies tranquility.
But sometimes,
    in times of change, there is a deeper need.
Esther and *Ezra*, when their people
    are at stake, take on roles
    otherwise suspect.
She is a maiden
    who becomes a sex slave to the foreign king.
He is a cupbearer who becomes
    an administrator higher than a prince.

In *Song of Songs*, two people were not allowed to wed,
    but seek to meet and make love.
2 Samuel. Among men love blooms.
An older prophet and a younger prophet
    walk the same road.
Their loyalty is tested.
United forever,
    amidst otherwise savage violence.

A taped page in this Bible
    where *Proverbs* meets *Ecclesiastes*.
It tends to fall apart there.
With fate, fortune, misshape, luck.
Desire meets dissolution.
Meaning meets meaninglessness.
Logical, dutiful
    competence competes with carnal,
    capricious, cynical resignation.

Ruth. Among women, new families
    are created, vows exchanged.
Love costs but survives amidst loopholes.

These stories are preserved as space. Not lines.
Yet lines help distinguish space.
The paradox of character.

A napkin from Winchell's Donuts falls
    out from between the pages.
He liked to go on Saturday mornings.

—

Such paradox surrounds mortal creatures
    in their worship of a transcendent God.
What about this God?
With God there is holiness and glory,
    righteousness and fear.
And with God there is also freedom
    and pleasure, passion, incarnation, and grace.

God in the Bible does not always command
    right and wrong.
Homeless Jacob wrestled with an angel.
Old Sarah laughed at one.
The LORD touched his hip
    until he walked with a limp.
The LORD took offense and she got childbirth.
Moses and God debated, dialogued,
    disagreed.
On occasion, a mortal changed God's mind.
Aaron did the same to Moses, challenging his authority.
Unlike leprous Miriam, Aaron's posture
    of dispute was honored, or at least forgiven.

God changed Pharaoh's mind, and changed
    it back, and changed it again—
    but took 400 years to do so.
Whereas Gideon put God to the test,
    and God showed up instantly to oblige.
Wonder-working prophets with strange reputations
    asked to walk with God all the way up to heaven.
And did!
Wayfarers pined for God and never saw.

—

There are two books in the Bible where God
    is barely mentioned.
Nothing about God can be controlled.
Nor contrived.

A thunderstorm you can't touch
    becomes humus you can smell.
That's what I like about rain.

—

I've asked myself, which character of God
    do I long for?
The reliable goal
    who holds mortals accountable in the end.

Or the capricious source on whom everything
      everything everything can be blamed.
The answer depends on story.
This or that is not the only.

—

A linear force with law and spear to enforce it.
Or the cyclical ground holding everyone in the round.
Everyone born must die.
And how is that an answer?

Even me and my dad, in a circle of forgiveness.

—

He died with his hands over his face.
I don't know why.
It was like they were crawling
      over him to conceal his eyes
      or to devour something demonic.
Maybe his hands were flung up to keep us out.
For, in truth, we were ready to forgive
      and love him. I think we were.
We did.
But he never let us in.

All he had to do was take his meds.
What he wouldn't do was take his meds.
Denial and disintegration.
Addled mental state, cognitive decline,
    conspiracy theories.
Which meant more denial.
Off meds, he was bad itchy. That too.
In the hospital room he covered his face
    with his hands and yelled
    when the psychologist came to visit.

—

He was a builder, a contractor, a carpenter.
All his working life.
This character, my dad.
Charming and generous enough to pass
    for a saint.
Prejudiced and conditioned to abuse.
Dreamed dreams of schemes
    to make money.
Some plans were fragile,
    some backfired, but some gave lasting happiness.
He worked to pay for his kids' dreams.
Left a pile of debt.
But he loved babies.

There's that part to the story.
In that one instance he never
      read the script of masculinity, or threw it out.
He held me in his hands and taught me to stand.
My dad loved my little ones,
      his grandchildren.
Cradled and cooed them endlessly, cuddled and sang.

He sang like rain.

When the grandbabies needed something,
      he rebuilt their nursery floor.
On hands and knees, while listening to Rush Limbaugh,
      while his condition deteriorated.
I looked on, between changing diapers.
One day the work stopped. He fell.
I helped him up.
I offered him my hands.
No lullaby, but a living collision.

Have you ever noticed we close our eyes to cry?
Like we close our eyes to pray.

Neuropathy in his legs, he said.
He said he did not want to live.

—

Look for purity in the Bible, and you will find it.
But you will also find poison in that cup.

Jesus danced with the chalice carefully.
He weighed in on morality when a woman
    was caught, when men were in control.
He got the aggressors to back off, stand down.
He weighed in when the disciples asked
    what a eunuch is worth.
Those with crushed testicles were the favorite,
    he said, in the kingdom of heaven.
He weighed in on a theology of purity
    and punishment.
That's not why the Tower fell!
Jesus and the naked disciple.
Jesus and the prostitute.
Jesus and his reputation for sharing a meal.
He taught love of neighbor, love of God.
Self-negation for the rich,
    self-affirmation for the poor.
He challenged the teaching of fathers,
    blessed the mystery of their children,
    touched the unclean,
    told the righteous to repent,
    and helped everybody feed each other.

Lessons and teachings.

Stories and miracles.

Jesus wound up crucified on a violent Roman cross.

Which God raised him up again?

WATER

My childhood secrets revealed, with missing pieces

Water. Land.
One of these elements cannot begin
    without the other.
Spring floods and pooling.
Insects and critters.
Sounds of life.

—

The story that I know begins,
    like all human stories, wet.
A slimy baby body born with huge, bright labia.
Placed into her mother's arms, father
    looking on.
There was joy and pride.
They gave the child
    a name from the Bible.
The name of one who looked on
    from the rushes as Moses floated
    downstream in a basket on the Nile.

The responsible sister.
This baby would become their middle child.
Known for prayerful intuition, second sight, devout.
Exultant in *Exodus,* telling of triumph and rescue
from slavery.

—

And then there are mountains.
That's where I come in really.
After rainbows. After rain.
The sky and clouds, peaks and valleys played
with me.
I played in the creek, in and under trees.
I grew suspicious of a "she."
I distanced from other people that way.
I read books with tom-boys and cross-dressers in them.
Later I heard the word "gay."
That sounded close.
Sometime after that I heard the word "transgender."
These words I heard did not sound God,
laughing in the morning
and in the evening, filling the sky
with every hue and shade at once.
But they were close enough to be true.

I was afraid.

I should tell you about the smell of granite.
From the garden of Eden to the metaphorical
    New Jerusalem.
From mountain to rock to cornerstone.
From canyon to high-rise.
And back again.
This is the story of water.

—

Fountains flowed past *Genesis* and *Psalms*,
    Ezekiel and *Amos, Joel.*
Wherever the rivers flowed were trees.
"The leaves of the trees were for the healing
    of the nations." *Revelation 22*

My rivers flowed, sparkling over fool's gold,
    a hundred years after the gold rush.
My father was smitten with the rivers.
And the mountains.
He came from Florida on his way to the wild west.
His daydream paused in Denver.
He settled.
When he saw the Rockies, he knew
    he could live there, lucky enough.
He married a woman.

According to script, had children.
Moved the whole family to elevation.

The smell of continental granite,
   gray and silver with mica.

"O mortal, what does the Lord require of
   you?" *Micah 6*
But to collect rocks, shiny and beautiful,
   and to admire them in a collection
   in the fort in the trees
   where no one else can come
   because no one knows about it.
A shelter, as they say.

No reason had I to be afraid.
But I did not know that.
Phobia is contagious.

"Lord, you have been our dwelling place
   throughout all generations." *Psalm 90*
This is a story of generations.
Literature that links us together.
Genres.
A library can hold my father's story.
And mine.

He was born-again from the radio.
From a best friend Baptist preacher.
No wayward path for him.

I was born born-again, and had to rebirth
    twice more.

I knew pine, juniper, and yucca by scent.
My fig trees, grapes, and olives
    were ink drawings in a King James Bible
    he gave to me.
Quartz and geodes were my fascination.
How do all those crystals come to be?
Clearly a process. And not at all clear.
Clear was the water in the cold, cold stream.
Colder than the melted snow
    which lasted until June.
My birthday. A day to go barefoot.
But not shirtless.

Listen to my father yelling at the TV
    on the day of a rainbow parade.
Contamination was coming, spoiling his dream.
I'm sorry, I wanted to tell him.
Perhaps he heard his father yelling.
Perhaps his father heard the church.

Rainbows were now forbidden.
Earrings for boys, Barbie dolls, and high heels trashed.
Lawn mowing and wood-chopping
    and working on cars were reserved,
        preserved from me.
Something threatening made it so.

—

The same land my father claimed
    as an immigrant, was indigenous centuries before.
Then came Spanish landowners and Xican laborers.
Why complicate this story with all others?
The Bible tells me so.
About the widows, the immigrants,
    indigenous.
Landowners and laborers.
Jonah, Ruth worried about them. Elijah,
    Nathan, did too.
And Jesus.
"Do not deprive the alien, the fatherless,
    or widow." *Deuteronomy 24*
"Do not take advantage of each other." *Leviticus 25*
"Proclaim liberty throughout the land
    and to all its inhabitants." *Leviticus 25*
"What do you mean by grinding
    the faces of the poor? Declares the LORD." *Isaiah 3*

"Woe to those who deny justice
     to the innocent." *Isaiah 5*

It's history. It's present.
The same rain.
Colonizer, victim of colonization, colonized.
Assimilated victim, colonizer.
High males on ladder rungs.
Everyone else beneath.

—

My father worked for people with money.
He tried to get respect. And money.
For that he hired Mexicans
     who had no money and who got no respect.

My father.
He had a soft spot for the individual.
The beaten-down boy, the rejected son,
     the lad who reminded him of himself.
He would hire him and try
     to teach him about money.
He befriended a gay man and tried
     to teach him about sin.
That's where his story changed.

—

Someone said God was an ugly master,
　　that sinners had to die of AIDS.
Something else said you are who you are.
Sexuality is a gift.
My father held it all. At once.
His God, his patriarchy, and his lovers.

The family never knew,
　　until we knew his HIV status from my mother.
He did not speak of it.
By then he had disowned us.
The children he was so proud of at birth.
For whom he dreamed his dream,
　　moved to elevation, to wash their feet
　　in mountain water.
He cut his children off
　　with words like "queer."
Recompense. A wicked equation.
He could not be inconsistent
　　with annihilation.
So he did not take his medicine.

He died a few times from pneumonia.
In hospitals they brought him back.
Compassionate gay doctors in big cities
　　trained in science and healing.

Women doctors and foreigners.
All the people he forgot about or judged.
They did not have the luxury to do the same.

And then he did die.
One last time.

—

My father's Bible—I kept it.
My feeling is this:
The widows, immigrants, orphans
    and laborers, also the eunuchs, centurions,
    vineyard owners, and emperors still need it.
Bible as broker of water.
From birth to grief.
From wealthy to poor.

Justice reflects a blue sky poured
    on the surface of a still pond,
    with green things growing lustrous
    beneath a generous yellow sun.
Orange fronds and purple peaks linked
    by downpour, until the grains come up.
All the injured of this earth need liquid
    flowing through our bodies.

Hydration.

So that mercy can be stunning, running red
like blood.

LEADERSHIP

Generations of influence on my dad, his funeral

To wear my dad's gloves felt
    different from little kids' gloves.
Meant for real work.
Warmth. Not a little warmth layer but a lot.
Meant for keeping out weather.
Weight. Not thin.
Durable grip.
Meant for swinging tools on a job site.

What he did.
What he didn't do.

I didn't hear his voice often.
He was soft-spoken.
He listened to talk radio.
Big men, bully pulpits, blowhard voices.

When I was little—that's a good one.
When I was little, he would tell me bedtime stories.

That time he ran from an alligator
  in the swamp.
That time his mother yelled
  at him for swatting mosquitoes in his hair
  when his hands were covered in green paint.
That time he set a fire by mistake.
That time his brother went for a gun
  to shoot a rat in the house.
His voice would lilt and drawl and stretch and laugh.
I fell asleep to the soft voice, a gentle backrub
  if I asked.

He told no stories about his father.

—

Patriarchs.

One time he raised his voice so I would pay attention.
Is that what his father had done?
"—or I will break every bone in your body!"
The words "black and blue" came out of his mouth.
The rest did not make sense to me at age four.
Or now.
I had wanted not to wear a dress.
My aunt made the dress. It was my birthday party.

I did not want to wear the dress. I said so.
He meant me to understand I had to wear
   the dress.

Patriarchs in the Bible are credited most.
But before patriarchs, it was matriarchs.
They did the matching, the deciding.
Politically they made things happen.
When they died, they were mourned as leaders.
This changed somewhere.
After that, Abraham was mentioned alone.
Not Sarah.

My dad's Bible underlined David, the good king.
Wasn't every man supposed to be a good king?
He tried.
Even the unfaithful part.

My dad's Bible underlined Moses, the leader.
The Ten Commandments.
Wasn't every man supposed to lay down the law?
And he did that.

My dad's Bible underlined Gideon, the warrior.
"Samson's strength." *Judges 6*

Law, goodness, use of force.
Somewhere striving to maintain innocence,
  my father got lost.
In his mind.
A soft-spoken man who loved babies.
He raged from little influence,
  little authority, little power.

He took us to hear preachers.
Sometimes he would hold forth at the dinner table.
My older brother would argue back.
Was it Eve, or was it Adam?
My younger brother watched. I listened.
We learned this was dangerous.
Like Saul who turned on his own family,
  who threw a spear after a banquet.

Jonathan was also underlined in my dad's Bible.
This is the sad part.
Lover of David, son of Saul.
Nobody wanted to be Jonathan.
He shot good arrows, but he was beheaded in battle.
"And David wept the most." *I Samuel 20*

In the retelling it went like this:
Whoever was emasculated couldn't be a
  good leader.

And girls must wear dresses.

—

With dress code he had a problem.
It meant men had to wear suits.
He swore those Southern Baptists up and down
    when they dismissed him for deacon
    because he didn't have a suit.
He knew how to budget very little,
    and how to go into debt a lot.
He stopped me from accepting a low-wage job.
Though that's the only kind he had, out of
    high school.
He was proud of me when I graduated college.
He bought me a good winter coat, and hat and gloves.

—

The men on TV and the men on the radio
    kept selling him things.
He bought everything they sold.
They sold gender roles. He bought them.
They sold financial advice. He bought it.
With their help, he could game the system.
Win the market.
Rise in a pyramid.

Not just build but profit from real estate.
They were his leaders.
He gave allegiance.
It didn't help.

They were Moses. He was *Joshua*.
They were Paul. He was *Titus*.
They were *Proverbs*.
He was no one's fool.

—

My dad never underlined Deborah or Jael.
Gender-transgressing women who led
    in government and battle.
Like others before him, he left off apostolic
    Mary, to highlight *Peter*, Paul, and *James*.

Tales of patriarchs got much louder
    than the lesson about eunuchs.
No matter Jesus' interruption of the family tree.

—

The preacher at my dad's funeral
    was a small man who wore an alb.

This pastor did not know him.
But he knew the 20th century.
The life men were expected to live.
And he knew a word of grace.
Which was all my righteous dad ever needed.

A man who speaks grace in a soft voice—
    can this be a man?

That is not my question.

—

After I transitioned, I came out to my family.
I had harsh words for my dad.
I wrote them in a long letter.
He kept my letter in the household safe
    with a code for a lock.
Nothing else was in there. Only that.
We found the letter after his funeral.

I was sad I had not given him my soft words.
Maybe I did—but
    those are not the ones he kept.

I wrote an obituary.

My mother wasn't sure she wanted a funeral.
It went unpublished.

—

When my father did buy a coat, it was a good coat.
Mid-life, when he had money.
He bought a good coat that lasted him well.
The rest of his life.

When I wear my father's coat now, I throw
    my shoulders back.
A heavy coat, rigid and impermeable.
I dare the wind.
It doesn't answer.

A still, small voice answers.
That is all.

—

Would my dad have come
    to hear me preach? I'll never know.
Some are attracted to the leader Saul.
A tall man, deep voice.
Odds are, he would take someone else down in battle.
Humiliate him. Keep the throne.

But I always loved that story about God
    looking on the heart.
God's prophet rejected Saul, and picked
    the runt instead.
That would be David. With a slingshot,
    the boy/femme/feminine/homo/queer defeated the
    giant/bully/braggart/manly/man.
My dad loved the story about David dancing before
    the Lord.

I never saw my dad dance as a child.
He wasn't the flaming, performing, closeted-
    to-no-one-but-himself kind.
Didn't play with pigskin.
Would have nursed a lamb.

The songs that David wrote—*Psalms*—
    are filled with self-indictment,
    prostration, abnegation.
Serious awareness of sordid wrongs.
But they generally reject vain princes.
Everyone has their limit.

I rejected the pulpit Goliaths, Bible
    thumpers, hawkers of spiritual abuse.

—

I came out, and went to seminary.
I didn't know I would become a pastor.
Missionary, maybe.
The secular equivalent:
    non-profit advocate/case worker/
    grant writer/public speaker.
I went to the forsaken zones of cities.
Found other trans people.
Found leaders.
The choir director who once lived under a bridge.
The alcoholic who ran a group.
The women who started Planned Parenthood.
The artists who painted graffiti.
The kind who held each other when
    somebody died.
Cast-offs become anchors.

No dress code at seminary.
They got to know me at the bookstore.
That's the first place I
    changed my name.
I bought lots of Bibles.
The thick kind with notes. Essays, even.
But no handwriting.
I added some.

My dad, like me, say the creased thumb-
    crescent-sticker pages of the Old Testament,
    didn't like Saul.
We both thought Solomon was ok.
My dad bought a big book of wisdom once.
It sat on our coffee table.
It had a special string through the binding,
    and stiff brown pages.
It must have been special.
Like *Proverbs*.
Do right, good stuff happens.
He marked every page of proverbs.

I had several jobs, while pursuing wisdom in seminary.
At the hospital, as a chaplain,
    they asked me to wear a tie.
Who wears a tie?
No one I knew.
Not my dad.
Not trans activists.
Not the women.
Not Jesus.
What class idolatry was this?

—

Mary and the matriarchs got their own books.
But theirs were left out of the canon.
Julia, Lydia, Priscilla and Aquila,
    other benefactors of the apostles.
Good Greek women.
Had they known the Wisdom tradition?
Maybe even leadership.
Christian women were the first to lead worship,
    raise their hands in prayer,
        eyes to heaven, bare feet on earth.
They gathered the community in catacombs.
Birthed life out of death.
Like cosmic midwives.
    they brought back the way-back ways.

Until the empire needed soldiers,
    when Constantine recruited Christians.
Boys, boys, boys.

Men held meetings, preached and preached.
But they didn't feed the people.
She did that—Christ, I mean.
And the trans woman who mothered many
    children while being persecuted state to state.
She fed the people too.
When I met her, she was an aging church-
    choir lady who would drop the F-bomb.

When she met me, she told me I would become a pastor.
Trans and a pastor?
I said I did not have it in me to be a scandal.
She said, "You be you."

That's why she was a good mom.

—

Titus worried about doctrine to define.
And who to call a heretic.
These tiny New Testament books from my dad
    have way more markings than the Gospels.
More sermons heard in person when he went to church.
He took good notes.
On more than one page, a list describing leaders.
It all came down to gender.
My dad tried to act like everything on that list.
Not greedy. Trustworthy. Good husband.
Good father to good children.
God, he tried for us to be good children.

Everything James Dobson said to do, he did.
Lay down the law.
Break the high heels.
Pray the gay away.

Rid me of the tractor.
But he accidentally taught me how to drive.
And he let me be in theater.
He showed me how to keep the books,
    and taught me to speak up when I
    was getting ripped off.

—

My granny was a good mom too.
As was my mom.
Both taught Sunday School.
Timothy, who learned the scriptures well,
    cited his grandmother Lois, and his mother, Eunice.
They knew more than scripture.

Esther was a queen in a court ruled by eunuchs.
There was a king, but his thing
    was getting drunk and throwing tantrums.
The eunuchs were the ones who knew
    what was going on.
The book never says they wanted to be eunuchs.
But—like priests and prostitutes—
    a courtier role earned them a third space
    apart from the rules of gender, sex, and marriage.

Teacher—that's good.
But maybe pastor. A third space.
Maybe pastor could be a catacombs thing.
Sacraments with the weak, with the poor.
With anointing oil.
Heads raised high.

—

My dad objected to seminary of the kind
    that would have me.
We spoke only in anger,
    so we learned not to speak.

I needed seminary to de-program reels of wrath.
The Bible is mutiny, not mercenary.

When I graduated, he did not come.

When I was ordained, he came,
    but closed his eyes.

GODS

Theologizing, making meaning, making babies

"For God so loved the world …" *John 3*
She did the begotten thing over and over
    and over again.
Of course this is heresy.
But some heresy is good for you.
Eat your vegetables.

What kind of father would I be?

It was just an idea.
Trans men having children was not famous yet.
I was not interested in a certain sense of self
    reduplicated.
Nor did I love to dote on other people's young.
I skipped babysitting in my don't-treat-me-
    like-a-girl phase.
I read dictionaries instead.

What happened was I met someone along
    my journey.
She very much loved me.
I very much loved her.
She knew she wanted children.
I said they're made of stardust.
With research and collaboration,
    we could do this. And we did.

This is slightly ahead of the story.
Before parenthood, was my re-baptism
You're not supposed to do that.
That's why you have to.

Should I hope this for you?

—

Far outside a church building,
    elemental forces.
Test and contest.
Sometimes with words.
Sometimes not.
Stories knit together.
Patterns connect, open up, connect again.

You will understand someday.
"The kingdom of God is within you." *Luke 17*

—

What they mean when they say "the grace of God."
Theological hinges. Interventions.
The person who took me in
    after another person kicked me out.
A pastor who sent me chamomile tea
    through the mail.
A congregation that fed me
    out of their food shelf,
    and taught me to laugh again.
A sense of humor is a big miracle, after all.

I pray you will. I pray they will.

Homeless, I found my next teachers of the
    sacred text.
All the translations and all the interpretations.
The ones people staked their lives to.
And the ones that burned others at the stake.

Making a home is a process,
    said my teachers.

Heard into healing around a kitchen table,
    said my teachers.
A shrine to the ancestors. A drum.
That's the Bible.

The conversation goes on.
You will make your own understanding.
Choices and commitments.
Re-readings.
With our words we reach.
Not altogether unconvinced that our words
    might reach something real by accident.
Something older than words.
Even older than breath.

Earth and sky are porous to each other.

Not just pollen.
Not just the floating, whirling, drifting matter
    that comes down and covers everything
    and becomes part of the dirt.
Not just the spaces found when you dig
    something up.
Something else which allows
    oxygen-fixing roots to thrive in soil.

—

Breathing mud, let's make breathing mud
    in our image, said God(s).
The narrative had fixed firmament and sky apart.
Now they mingle.
Interpenetrate.
Let's give breathing mud a companion, said God(s).
This is how it starts.

Who is this God(s)?
All the names of God in the Bible.
Commander of the angel armies.
Many-breasted one.
Bull sculpture.
Asherah poles. The poly deities of Egypt.
The stars of Zoroaster.
The goddesses of the Mediterranean world.
From the statues in Rome that had names,
    to the Hebrew unnamed unnamable.
Which names of god were god?

Was anything not god, once?

—

The Bible is a mash-up of cultures.
The most unpronounceable things are not the names
    of God, but the names of groups.

If it ends in "ites" or "eans" or "ians" or "ans,"
    that's a people.
They didn't believe the same things.
They had disputes because they wanted to be right.
Right about the stars
    and the cycles for planting.
Right about worship and fertility, and right
    about heirship.
Right about moral codes or social class or
    legal codes.
Rules made sacrosanct by somebody.

That which you worship is your God,
    a preacher once explained.
We all worship something.
Worshiping is what breathing mud is made for.

—

Dandelions breathe too, and snapdragons.
Johnny jump-ups.
And mushrooms.
Algae and oaks breathe.
"Let everything that has breath, praise the
    Lord!" *Psalm 150*
The preacher may or may not have explained this.

—

How to say it.

Theology, per Jesus:
The tower of Siloam didn't fall
    because people were bad.
In other words, no selfish, interventionist God.
You can be a profligate prodigal problem
    and also be embraced.
A counter-intuitive God.
Close enough to see the sparrow fall,
    and to clothe the lilies of the field.
But not identical to those things.
Panentheistic, transcendent God.
Not evil.
But also capable of leading toward or away from evil.
Holistic.
A forgiving God.
But only if God's people also practiced forgiveness.

I kept this God.
This God kept me.

—

A THEO you can be mad at, who all
    the same might save your life.
An INCARNATE SPIRIT

with passionate emotion and moral
   imagination.
With flair for Beatitudes and parables
   and invisible realms and outrageous math
   where everything equates.
!=<~>?!

"Blessed are the poor in spirit." *Matthew 5*
The first red letters my father marked.
Ever and always they catch my attention.

Jesus found me thinking about God
   underneath the pollen and the pinecones.
Suggested we take a walk, shaped like a cross.
He gentled the epistles.
Upstaged the Gospels.
Invited me to recover and to rise.
Move forward.
And turn again.

My dad was a good storyteller.
Twinkles in his eyes.
Generosity too.
His prayers started, "Father,"
   but that did not mean what it meant.
His father was not God.
It takes a lifetime to know that.

My mother was the one who said yes,

    she would come to my queer wedding.

She stayed with my father but not his ways.

She first held my babies.

She sang to them.

Abba-God is gender-everything.

You can love this God with heart, soul, mind,

    strength, and affirmation.

With insecurity, uncertainty, courage,

    raw desire, and speechlessness.

That God.

For awe and devotion.

For death and for life.

For wonder and learning.

For flesh and bone.

For paradox and celebration.

For tongue and belly.

Skin and womb.

For love.

One GOD.

—

There are other options.
Contested but conversely respected in the Bible.
A different stroke drawing immanent
    and transcendent forms.
Rational it isn't but is.
Tribal it is but isn't only.

A God of laws and the reformation of laws,
    who implored humans in community
    to do the work of discernment.
A God of miracles.
Resurrection, for example.
Which did not precede but followed
    adoration of the cranky, smiling, hungry,
    lonely, hopeful, merciful carpenter-turned-
    spiritual-leader whom breathing mud
    creatures called affectionately: "Lord."

—

My secret power.
To breathe the wind under the trees.
To realize I'm still here.
To heal.

My tears at Christ's communion table
    were my calling.
I was surprised.

I was ordained.

My racial biography continued: here
    and there, in-between.
Privileged to drive anywhere, to live
    anywhere, to move.

I was not always employed.
But I had resources.
Anger aged me.
Kindness grew me.
I found belonging in each new place.

—

My dad's stories turned to conspiracy theories.
His brain damage turned to paranoia.
His anger from a wheelchair consumed him.
Like a prophet raining fire on Baal, his
    lightning strike was misdirected.
My father was not comforted by any vanquishing.

Humans have our flaws.
We like to cast them skyward.
Authoritarianism, for instance.
We want Santa to have two lists.
True. False.
Binary with no null.
Power dynamics.
Male–female.
Dome over plate.

But Gehenna's fires do not balance out
    a feast in the end.
The feast wins.
All are invited, from south and north
    and east and west.
No need to apologize, sanitize, stabilize,
    theorize, or summarize.
But reverence.
Imagine.
Endeavor.
Give, receive, relate.
Survive and overcome.

—

A dragon god. That's in there.
Dictators made it hard to critique
	the hegemon.
So *Revelation* wrote in code.

A hemisphere away, Mayan priests believed
	in the end of time.
So do half of physicists.
Whatever the theology of an era, look for
	lots of theologies in lots of people.
Rituals and alternative rituals.
One person might contain multiple beliefs.
Every prophet sings multiple songs.

—

My father tried to crack the code.
His end-times predictions did not agree.
They missed the point, unless the point was fear.
I threw them out.
I had had enough of fear.
The voice of Jesus said:
Be not afraid.
Do not be frightened.

Amazement worked for me.

All humble in the clear bright light
      of the universe, I realized I could not tell
      my Creator how I was supposed to be.
My part was to be.
And that is mystery.

I've been drawn to mystics ever since.
"Fear not." *Mark 5*

—

A warm campfire on a chill night is a good way
      to leave the freeze for a thaw.
Let the seasons change.
Get some rest.
Until dawn awakens you.

Theology is a question, an endless conversation.
Ideology is imposed at different times.
For ideology, any deity will do.
Idols are whatever takes you over
      so you have nothing left to give.

My dad gave himself to something
      that took his life.
It was not God.
It was certainty and social norms.

In relationship with GOD, reflection.
The Bible is a map of life
    after exploration has been made.
A survey of keepsakes from a journey.
It can't tell you how you feel,
    but sometimes you recognize the landmarks.

The Books of Wisdom are like
    the adolescent books that throw
    all that theology back, test it all, take it
    apart, throw it in someone's face.
I like the Books of Wisdom.
Crude and elegant.
Oh, really? *Ecclesiastes* seems to say.
Ooh, baby—Song of Songs.
Job compresses the whole story
    of the Israelites and all possible takes on it.
Is suffering the last word?
Or were the *Psalms* and *Proverbs* right,
    do evil people get their due,
    and the righteous flourish forever?

—

The seasons turn.
Lament becomes a lullaby.

Either we turn to each other, or we turn away.
Or both.

—

Who you choose, chooses you.
Rejoice, revere, respect, rely on.
The redeem part is hard.
It must have been for Jesus.
Taking what is, and making what could be.
Even when what is hurts so much.

The church invents a metaphor:
Father, Holy Spirit, Son.
It's not exactly in the Bible.
Father is there—she's the one searching
    her whole house looking for a waylaid coin.
Spirit is there—they're the one working
    miracles of life.
Son is there—but he acts more like a mother,
    parenting the flock like a hen,
    feeding the young from his body.

From New Testament polyamory,
    perichoresis, derived the Trinity,
    a bizarre philosophy, for sure.

Written after Scripture
    about the heavenly side of an earthly God.
Arrogant to codify.
But it takes humility, doesn't it?

Millions of moments of millions of people
    relating to self and ALL IN ALL
    in a multiverse of meanings.
To pray. Beyond right or wrong.
To locate a particular practice of heart
and breath in bravery and beyond.

There is a wildness to God's love.
Provocation.
The faith didn't belong to my dad.
But he belonged to it.

Friends.
Lineage.
So many experiences kept leading me
    in this language.
Tensions. Wounds and salve.
Being right was never an option.
Recognizing a path was.

These spiritual currents do not belong to us.
I belonged to something my body knew.

Past sense and story.
Cycling from adventure to home, and back **again**.
Wider and wider circles of belonging.

—

The words my dad read were not always
　　the same words he pronounced.
He read Jesus saying, "Love one another.
　　as I have loved you." *John 13*
He wrote down: UNNATURAL.
He read how Jesus undid death,
　　but he wrote down an open question.
"More than that. Adam was created
　　for earth—not only for heaven—
　　something to think about?"

It matters if Jesus
　　doles out escape-from-hell vouchers or
　　shows us solidarity on earth.
It matters if God the Spirit is there
　　to regenerate, restore, renew, reform,
　　recompose, recycle, recapacitate us,
　　call us beyond our current selves.
It matters if we see ourselves
　　in relation to Creator and creation.

—

Repent is a word worth keeping.
"Which of you, if your child asks for bread,
    will give a stone instead?" *Matthew 7*

Tradition is a library of lives.
A treasure trove of treason and union.
Brothers at war, as in *Obadiah*.
Long memories of pain and retribution.
Embraces awaited.

My dad gave what he had.
Snake stew. And alligator stories.
Homophobia, racism, sexism too.

Each person is a book, perhaps a love poem.

A church keeps family photo albums.
The child united with a prodigal father.
The wanderer who finds home.
The captive freed.
The exile found.
Stories continue.

—

My babies were baptized
　　　on a sparkly Sunday morning in Colorado.
Their mother sang. I played guitar.
You might remember or forget
　　　the lyrics to that song.

I gave what I had.

Part Three

"Is it not written?" *Mark 11*

HOW THINGS SHOULD BE?

My queer place in ministry

Looking back, I was sure trees should grow straight.
Never the gnarly, the jagged, the swirled,
    asymmetric, the weirdly bent.
Always the totally vertical ones, standing alone.
Exemplars!
But trees all over do grow bent, angled, split,
    straddled, gnarled, spiraled, split and braided,
    heaved and stretched.
Crusted, hollowed, regrown off-kilter.
Whole forests grow in great variety.

Some trees fall down.
Some make way.
Some just let go.

—

"Honor your father's God," is not scripture.
"For the Bible tells you so," is not scripture.
Listen to see.

My father held his Bible close.
He marked the thin and crinkly pages.
These pages taught me his handwriting—
    block letters.
Heavy, so it might go through.

Three things I notice.
In ink.
The plan of salvation.
No confession.
No absolution.
Four: How hard it was for him to forgive
    himself.

—

I have a minister's stole with a tree on it.
It is a twisty tree.
A prayer for peace.

Seminary led to a way of life.
Activism, art, faith community.
Transgenerational legacy.

I have worn my stole where humans live
    and die, are born and age, sup and kill.

Where people have turned toward
    and turned away from divine inheritance.

—

His Bible opens at the spine at *Romans*.
That's where the bookmark is.
Marking the place.
A book that divides God's law from grace.
Though it was trying to splice, not slice, the two.

Splice.
That's what you do in a nursery.
My dad would know.
That was the children's job.
They would take cuttings.
They would graft.

But converts divide.
Before and after.
Changes everything.
Hebrews, for example, isn't.

Ribbon bookmark, black, for "the wages
    of sin is death." *Romans 6*
Pay attention to wages, he taught me.
Make sure you're getting paid fairly.

The immigrants who found nursery jobs were
Black and Brown.

The weight of leaves when they fall, adds up.

—

The oddest part of the Bible.
The weirdest part.
Not that Paul bought Onesimus' freedom,
manumitted as a full man from a slave-owner
named *Philemon*.
Not how slavery was part
of the Roman empire's plebeian system.
Not how rich men always profited from
poorer men.
That's not strange.

But how caste was simultaneously rejected
and held up by the church.
While others did their mischief in between.
A woman merchant named Lydia
has no husband mentioned.
She wore purple.
A certain man carried jugs of water.
Queer.

Queer meant in and alongside, for me.
In between and both.
Now and future.
Church as it could be, should be, and is.
My calls to serve were in neglected places.
Disgraced. Discarded. Disregarded.
"Hear this, ye who trample the needy
    and do away with the poor of the land." *Amos 8*
"What does the Lord require of you?
    but to do justly and to love mercy
    and to walk humbly with your God." *Micah 6*

—

Now a scuffle.
On the one side, preserving religion
    and culture, the best of what came before.
On the other side, emissaries trumpeting
    in *Corinth*, *Galatia*, *Philippi*—how religion
    and culture were overcome
    by a faithful way of life.
The Bible off the edge of a map.
Law and grace inverted.
Christians said the latter and meant the former.

In a certain translation, the year I was born,
    homosexuals among the damned.

Handwriting: It's in the genes.
Little black thumb stickers on the semicircle
    cutouts near the right edge of the page.
Glinting metallic edges.
So many shades of rust and gold.

All trees lose their leaves, but not all seasonally.
Structure and restructure are the vital force.
Tradition too.

Hope? Good? Glory?
No, my dad distilled a toxic sap
from *Romans*.
Boiled down, concentrated guilt.
A stain of egg literally on the page.
Residue of a breakfast plate.
Putrid, rotten court appearance no one can pass.
Life? Learning? Growth?
Not on the menu.

—

How did Sarah think things should be,
    when Abraham had a picnic with a few
    visitors under some oaks?
Had they no plan at all, but faith?

Homeless wanderers,
	they became progenitors of a fecund family tree.
No—several.

Maybe they wondered how things were
	supposed to be.
Maybe they were certain.

—

Who decides?
That's a question we are taught not to ask.
Like about money.
Either there's no point to talking about it
	because your people do not know.
Or your people are the ones who simply
	know, so there's no need to discuss it.

Joseph was my dad's favorite character.
Life threw him into a pit.
But he rolled with it
	and came out on top of a pyramid.
Take that, famine! Take that, oppressive economy!
Resentment of the rich.
Desire to be like them. To be them.

Joseph might have been queer.
Laws against it weren't written yet.

My dad would not have liked it if Joseph was queer.

—

Laws are like that.
One day they're not there; the next day they are.
U.S. borders move south over the Mexicans,
    north over the Acadians,
    west over the Hawaiians.
Colonial impasse in the Caribbean.
Rules create trespassers.

Who pays? Who benefits?
Who decides?

That's not how it's supposed to be.
White people, we love our law and order.
Except when God and guns work better.
One's a high-and-mighty thing, genteel.
One's a low-class thing for thugs.
Here's how it works:
    push somebody down and scramble over them.

Tricksters in scripture know the power game.

Crinkle shuffle.
Sweep.

—

Dad's handwriting, again:
"Convert others. Resist temptation."
And something about "abortion."
But Jesus said only one of these.

This curious note: "The opposite of play
    is depression. When we don't laugh,
    we lose our health!"

He had insomnia, my dad.
My mom cared for him until the end.

—

When the leaves go, you can see
    the shape of each tree trunk.
Each branch.
Up they go, toward the sun, toward
    the arc of the universe.

But each growth tells a story.
The story begins underground.
Its shape is a wiry mess.
By the time it gets high enough
 to have filaments in the sky, the form
 looks like a crooked skew of fractal feathers.
The only balance goes round and round,
 beneath, above.
Nothing two-dimensional.

Not even vistas at a distance.

LAND

At the graveyard, reminiscing in relationship, decolonizing faith

In the winter he would chop ice with an ax.
To see if it was thick enough for us to go ice skating.
After clearing the pond ice of snow,
    he dragged sleds of kids who wanted to go fast.
After watching us play, he would build
    a large bonfire on the shore.
Large enough to warm anyone ten feet away.
His eyes would light up with the smile
    his face was too cold to crack.
He had blue eyes.
He loved winter.

—

You already know his hero was Joseph,
    raised to power by Pharaoh.
Also David, named king by a prophet.
Take that, Goliath!

Both had humble origins, and found
    their fortunes reversed.
Work your way up.
Bootstraps.
Plus a miracle.

Other stories he underlined
    were promised-land stories.
Stories about the land.

The land he found to raise a family on
    had an upper pond, and a lower pond,
    with river coming off the creek.
(Hear "crick.")
He built a dam to control the flow.
He made sure the inlet was dug out every spring.
He gave the stream a name.

He built a small house, called a playhouse,
    near the creek, downhill from the big house.
That was for me—though I spent little time in it.
He built the family house from the ground up.
I watched him pour cement for a foundation,
    on top of spindly rebar tines.
He told me not to get too close or fall in.
He was watching out for me.

I watched him lay logs across each other
    to build a wall.
The angles met. The walls rose.
I watched him hammer plywood and shingles
    for a roof.
So fast! He swung his hammer.
One small ping, then wham.
Two swings were all it took to drive a nail.
He let me hammer long nails.
If I swung the hammer twenty times
    then I could get it through a board.
Many rooms in a big house.
Many blisters on my hands.

He carved his name on a sign of wood,
    and put the sign at the bottom of the driveway.
Big enough to be read a quarter mile away.
He put the apostrophe in the wrong place.
So it was singular.
It was his land.
None other's.

—

My father also loved the stars.
More than once appears the word "Astrology"
    scrawled on turned-down corners of a page.

A bad thing.
Penalized.
Would he get too close to the sky?

Abraham wandered from his father's land.
If he had not wandered, the rest
    would never have been written.
He went far.
But he wanted to settle down.
After placing competing claims,
    he and his relative parted ways.
Wandering. Settling.
Wandering some more.
Their sons would see stars. And angels.

"My father was a wandering Aramean." *Deuteronomy 26*
So says the confession.
Who else was there?
All the other Arameans.
All the other Canaanites.
All the others in the land.
The land was not empty.

—

It's easy to fall in love with land.
All you have to do is live there.
See sunrise, noonday, mid-afternoon,
     sunset, starlight.
See it again.
Through seasons of different insects,
     precipitation, storms, sickness, injury, trust.
Gain your food from it.
Learn how it provides.
Depend on it.
When you know you depend, you fall in love.
No water will ever taste as good.
No color of rock will ever be as solid.
No other sky the right height.

—

Written on page 758.
"Death—Why?"
Another corner turned down.
For future reference.

The land that was lost was not
     the same as that which was promised.
Mingle gratitude and regard, dependence and awe.
That's paradise.

159

But always ever after, there is someone
    to smite, and sweat on your brow,
    and the hard uncertainty of labor.

—

Abraham chose a good place to bury Sarah.
Under the landmark of a large tree.
The tree would outlive them all.
Abraham and Sarah's children kept going.
Until one day, they were hungry
They wandered into Egypt to avoid famine.
They had a hard time wandering out.
By then there were even more Arameans.
More people in the land.
Father Abraham indeed had many sons.
So now the promised land was occupied.
Was there land for everyone?
On what was based possession?

—

Everything American says turf is for claiming,
    digging, staking, mining.
Scalping. And moving on.

In grids spaced out with squares, settler
    colonizers started monoculture.
Then improved it with machinery.
What could be cultivated was extracted,
    leaving dust behind.
Grain grows. Grain dies.
Grain is meant to grow again.
But not with desertification,
    genetic modification, hyper-monetization.
It became possible not to fall in love with the land.
Not to depend.

But in some people lives paradise, so strong,
    they will build it with their own two hands.
On top of someone else, if they have to.

A street-level sign in my town marked whose
    it used to be.
People gathered there at the hot springs
    for peace talks. Once. More than once.
Peace was a regular achievement.
It took time to make and keep.
A statue marked who claimed the land.
A gold miner.
His tall statue stood on a boulder.
He had my father's father's haircut.

Probably blue eyes.
The gold rush came and went.
Then silver, molybdenum.
We learned how to say that word
    in elementary school.
On Miner Street.

We told stories about the land in English.
We did not know in Colorado that the land had
    heard other languages before.
Spanish. And before Spanish, the language of
    the Nuche.

My dad objected to any language but English.
He kept gold flecks in jars.
After some time, medicinal silver too.
By the time I wandered far from my father's house
    he had mercury and gems, herbs and crystals.
He credited homeopaths with keeping him alive.
Nearly dead.
Very broke.

A romantic myth.
Buying gold.

The railroad restarted a ghost town.

My dad came west with a hammer in his hand.
He would build custom log homes for
    modern settlers.

Employment and unemployment were hard
    to tell apart.
My dad's best prospects came when hired
    to manage a crew of laborers in a cabinet shop.
He found new immigrants who did good work.
My dad made money.
He took out a mortgage.
He could say he owned the land.
The workers made hourly wages,
    and rented small apartments together.

The Aramaic word for people of the land
    means not to mess with them.
They are in God's favor and God
    is their protector.
Even if they're poor.
Especially if they're poor.
"Anawim."
Which means not just the Israelites.

—

Taking care of the stranger was a commandment.
"For you too were strangers in the land
    of Egypt." *Exodus 22*
Nobody oppress anybody!
You ought to remember what it's like to be oppressed.

It takes time to make and keep the peace.

Remember the poor.
Look after the immigrant.
"What you did for the least of these, you did
    for me." *Matthew 25*

The way God talks about land: it's always contingent.
There is a covenant to respect.
If justice becomes injustice, and goodness
    nothing, and the poor mistreated,
    and the land worked to death,
    the promised deal is off!

God is in love with the land.

The land talks about God too.
Everywhere praise.
Glory on a thousand hills.
Faithfulness in fruit and olive trees.

The sun goes out of its chamber
    in the morning, and rides across the sky,
    and wherever it goes, God is.

The grain grows. The grain dies. The grain
    grows again.
Jesus blessed and broke it.

Earth is marked where it meets the sea.
Kind of.
Who can keep the tide in place?
Who can mark the line between the ocean
    and the shore?

There was a flood in *Zephaniah*.

They had built a wall in *Habakkuk*.

Ezekiel came through a valley, to foretell a river.

"Why do you speak to the people in
    parables?" *Matthew 13*
Make art from suffering.
Stories you can take with you.
Artifact, fact of art.

This Bible binding, for instance.

I can smell it.

GUARANTEED FOR LIFE
　　says an original coupon from a Mississippi
　　leather company, folded in the front cover.

—

The dam my dad built had to be rebuilt each spring
　　but he hasn't been there in years.

The upper pond became silt.

The lower pond washed away into the creek.

SUFFERING AND PRAISE

A ghost, forgiveness, and why I didn't die

Some leaves let go at night, apparently.
Nothing cerulean about it.
No vapor of sun.
No tinkle of eyesight
    to catch the batch of desiccated carbon.
They fall as one.
Then decay.

Unfirm.

Not like my father's hammer.
I hold the handle still in my hand.
Touching everything he was ever taught
    about being a man.

I wasn't taught how to use it.
Construction? Or deconstruction?
Always.

—

Funny about mourning. It goes on and on.
There is space for a while.
Then there is nothing
    in the space where something used to be.
The nothing changes.
Texture, weight and size.
It becomes solid in a trance.
An absence.
Then it melts.
As it melts it burns a space again.

To manage such a metamorphic, I say thank you.
For the brilliant autumn beauty.
Even though I know the beauty passes.
Before I finish this sentence more leaves
    will fall, and they will not rise again.

The steel of my dad's hammer
    bears rust that is red.

The space of the nothing has to have color,
    is what I'm saying.

—

God owes an explanation, thought the minor prophets.
All this suffering!
They made one up.

American Christian nationalists
    chose a color: white.
Blame the impure.
The foreigner.
The dissident. The feminist.
As though you belong because you are
    not one of them.
My father knew he was a Christian.
They told him that.
They did not say the rest.
He thought he was a patriot.

He never met a radical socialist transsexual.
Unless you count me.
I was taught to be a zealot.
Saving something important from someone.
Someone dangerous.
All this I had to unlearn.

Have to unlearn.

—

It must have hurt my dad,
    the day that I could see his faults.
I could not unsee them.
My eyes held seeing, not redeeming.
That must have been painful to his soul.
My ringing tones pounding his racism,
    class striving, misogyny, internalized
    colonized homophobia, religion
    weaponized for self-destruction.
My crude hammer of words.

This man bought me a winter coat.
Planted spring flowers with my mother.
Played in a summer pond.
Watered lilacs past their drift
    of scent and aspens
    until their shadows let go.

He closed his eyes to block out my seeing.

He left me with his ghost.

—

Seasons change.

He hurt.

Then he hurt me.

He said, when I was bold with rainbows,
"My, my, aren't my kids selfish."
Malforming words.
Like barbed wire.
A cable can cut to the heart of a tree.

Suicide would have been easier.
Did I mention that already?
The easiest outcome for a trans kid in the sticks.
Grown, but not open.
Alone, forlorn,
   confused, judged, ashamed as hell.
Condemned by heaven.

—

Now I consider my father.
How he took his life.

Job didn't, though.
Job with a long 'o'—sounds like woe.
A nice little book in the Bible.
They tell you not to read it because
   the metaphysic is so sick.

Satan and God, wagering on humankind.

How much can humans take?

A woman loses everything.

Her husband suffers.

They decide whether to praise or not.

Their suffering continues.

That's life. The allegory.

The upshot of outcast history.

Unlike the minor prophets,
    the main character parts with moralism.

There is no explaining why.

Unlike the major prophets, there is no happy ending.

Is there?

The major prophets help God out.

It's not God's fault.

It's our fault.

Human injustice as cause for divine revenge.

Consequences from atrocities.

Generations deep.

Zip codes of poverty
    for your children caused
    by what my ancestors did.

Now all our children will suffer.

We must work to get it right.
Yet human injustice
   as cause for divine revenge remains
   a strange interpretation.
Jesus said the sun shines, the leaves fall,
   for both the righteous and unrighteous.

Job just stares at the sun.
And the wind and the leaves.

I don't understand, he says finally.

—

Seasons change again.

—

Me, I also carry racism, sexism, internalized
   phobia, weaponized dominion.
Confession: I too want to avoid poverty.
I cannot tell religious reverence
   from wretched monuments.
Confession: On this planet I am selfish.
I see my own faults more and more.
I cannot unsee them.

Yet all kinds of hands have touched
    these hands of mine.
And none of them are nothing.
Only everything to learn from.

Angels have scribed in my palms
    words which are good words.
Words not only for me.
Words whether or not I am worthy:
    hope and joy and anger.
Water, life, place.
Encounter.
Reciprocity.
Words of relationship
    in lieu of retribution.

—

Reasons to praise.

The people will come back from exile.
God will proclaim comfort.
"Comfort, comfort, my people." *Isaiah 40*

Sometimes I like the if/then.
Your night will become like the noonday,

if you nourish the waters of justice,
   your roots will be well grounded.
There's something to that.
Logic.
The age-old foundations. Restored.

But the hereafter isn't clear.
The promise is present.

All of this creation came from the place
   a new creation will come.
From sky to earth and back again.
When the bent woman rises.
When the child dead gets up again.
When the wounded man heals.
When the hungry are filled.
When enemies are loved.

Even oneself.

—

My hands.
Foliage on nature's tree.
On loose leaf paper I trace sacred question marks.
My fingers hold folios of stories.

My chaff of breath and tears melt nothing
   into something again.
Words of life and death return from the void.

—

Discordance undid my dad.
Minor became major.
Breaking the yoke of marriage, he yet stayed in it.
Family law to preserve his seed.
His son betrayed the flag.
Failure. Guilt.
I say his death was suicide.
By moral trauma.
Or despair.

It was all too much.
My father didn't want his life anymore.
His less than able legs.
His fuzzy mind.
His regimen of meds.
His episodic pneumonia.
His bombastic radio.
His sordid son.
His blemished biography.

When the preachers came on, he slept
	in front of the TV screen.
Confused, alone, forlorn, ashamed.
When the rainbows came on, he spat.
Rebuked and repudiated them.
Called them dadgum liberals,
	out of their ever-loving minds.
A chaplain came to the hospital room.
Spoke of grieving.
Space for breaths and bravery.
Divine offer of acceptance.
He threw the chaplain out.
That was the day he died.

On the ash heap he chose.
Suffering without praise.

—

I tremble too but dance and laugh.
A mixed inheritance.

A holy Spirit. And the other kind.
A brutal crucifixion.
A blessed communion.

The end of so much.

The offer anew.

Small words.

Carbon.

Glory.

Story.

Sugar.

Skin.

Cup.

Gift.

Love.

Question.

How can I understand?

Yet I will praise my Maker.

Post-script

Cicadas screech and preach in time.
A cricket's castanet.

Time out of time.
Invites disorientation, decomposition,
   disintegration.
Fragmentation.

In *Hebrews* and *James* the elders argue about
   ancestors.
Did they live by faith or works?
They argue loudly with each other.

—

I had a dream about my dad.
He was thin but happy.
In his work truck we drove together
   to an old church where he now lived.

He was sexton and never preached.
He pointed. Didn't say much.
I recognized his gestures, his truck, his things.
We passed a day.
I was glad to be together.
I had a thought, by sunset.
There.
Is hope yet.

—

Metamorphosis.
Takes apart. Takes time.
Puts back together. Something new.

Cyclical.
Generational.
Quizzical.
Gestational.

—

And again it is autumn.
My life is older, rounder, nearer a bend.
Poetic tempo. Go and come.
I have hurt and healed.

Beat.

Pause.

A book, a scroll, a text marks a liminal space.

Enter through a portal, come out the other side.

Like water for a dragonfly.

Like earth for a beetle.

Like trees for cicadas.

We creatures go there when we need to heal.

Or transform.

Jesus quoted scripture and the earth.

Time after time.

Not a boundary to block out.

But ritual to enter in.

Notes

Allusions in this work to scripture passages are made with reference to the New International Version of the Bible, produced from 1965–1978 by an American group of evangelical church leaders, and published by Zondervan. The NIV has since become the most globally distributed translation to English-speakers worldwide. Copyright is held by the successor organization, Biblica.

Paperback cited in this text is *The Christian Life: New Testament with the Psalms, King James Version, with Master Outline and Notes Compiled by Porter Barrington*. Special Crusade Edition published for the Billy Graham Evangelistic Association (Minneapolis, MN: World Wide Publications, 1969).

Acknowledgments

As literary partners expanding the landscape for new voices, I would like to thank Jessica Powers, editor Fourie Botha, and the whole team at Flare Books. They took on a unicorn and treated this project with discernment and encouragement. As early readers of my work, several companions provided invaluable support for craft: Martie McMane, Shannon Kearns, Liam Hooper, Mac Herrling, Matt Powers, Mary Ylvisaker Nilsen, and Suzanne Woolston Bossert. Thank you to Jonathan Wilson-Hartgrove, Chanequa Walker-Barnes, and all of the Collegeville Institute Mystic Activists.

With deep gratitude I acknowledge mentors who, on their spiritual journey through life, have found ways to learn and grow from human traditions including family, identity and culture, through religious harm and religious healing. Lifetime thanks to Bill Johnson of the United Church of Christ and Major Griffin-Gracy, with whom it all started.